A Gift of

The Wellesley
Free Library
Centennial Fund

Macaws

By Erika and Jim Deiters

Raintree Steck-Vaughn Publishers

A Harcourt Company

Austin · New York
www.steck-vaughn.com

ANIMALS OF THE RAIN FOREST

Published by Raintree Steck-Vaughn Publishers, an imprint of Steck-Vaughn Company.

Library of Congress Cataloging-in-Publication Data
Macaws/Jim Deiters, Erika Deiters.
p.cm.—(Animals of the rain forest)
Includes bibliographical references (p. 31).
ISBN 0-7398-4682-5
1. Macaws—Juvenile literature. [1. Macaws.] I. Title. II. Animals of the rain forest.
QL696.P7 D45 2001
599.7'1—dc21

2001019822

Printed and bound in the United States of America
1 2 3 4 5 6 7 8 9 10 WZ 05 04 03 02 01

JUVENILE
598.71
Deiters

Produced by Compass Books

Photo Acknowledgments
Corbis/Michael & Patricia Fogden, 13; Steve Kaufman, 15. Digital Stock, cover. Ken Lucas, 24. Parrot Jungle, title page, 6; 28-29. Photo Network/Mark Newman, 8. Photophile/Anthony Mercieca, 22. Visuals Unlimited/Mary Morina, 11, 26; Barbara Magnuson, 16; R.F. Ashley, 18. Wildlife Conservation Society, 21.

Content Consultants
Cynthia Sims Parr, Content Development Director, Animal Diversity Web
University of Michigan Museum of Zoology

Maria Kent Rowell, Science Consultant, Sebastopol, California

David Larwa, National Science Education Consultant, Educational Training Services
Brighton, Michigan

This book supports the National Science Standards.

Contents

MEXICO

BELIZE
HONDURAS
NICARAGUA

GUATEMALA
EL SALVADOR Caribbean
Sea

COSTA RICA

PANAMA

ECUADOR

COLOMBIA

North
Atlantic
Ocean

GUYANA

VENEZUELA SURINAME

FRENCH
GUIANA
(FRANCE)

AMAZON
RIVER

PERU

BRAZIL

BOLIVIA

South
Pacific
Ocean

PARAGUAY

CHILE

South
Atlantic
Ocean

ARGENTINA URUGUAY

Range of the
Blue Macaw

Surrounding
Land

Water

Borders

Rivers

N
W   E
S

A Quick Look at Macaws

What do macaws look like?

Macaws are large and colorful birds. Their feathers are usually green, blue, red, and yellow. They have short necks and large rounded heads. They have thick, curved beaks and very long tails.

Where do macaws live?

Some macaws live in the rain forests of Mexico and Central and South America. They also live on islands off the coast of South America.

What do macaws eat?

Macaws eat nuts, berries, leaves, and buds. A bud is the part of a plant that grows into a leaf or flower. Macaws also eat food that other animals will not touch. They eat fruit that is not ripe. They even eat foods with toxins, or poisons, that would make other animals sick.

Macaws are colorful parrots that live in rain forest trees.

Macaws in the Rain Forest

Some kinds of macaws live in rain forests. Rain forests are places where many different trees and plants grow close together. A lot of rain falls in rain forests.

Macaws are the largest and most colorful members of the parrot family. The scientific name for this family is Psittacidae (sih-TAHS-uh-dee). It means to repeat something. Parrots are known for repeating what they hear.

Macaws are named after the macaw palm tree. The birds eat the nuts from this tree.

There are about 300 kinds of parrots. Their bright colors and voices have made them some of the best known birds in the world. Other members of the parrot family are parakeets and cockatoos.

Hyacinths are the largest kind of macaws. They were named after their purplish color.

Kinds of Macaws

Scientists think there are 17 macaw species. A species is a group of animals or plants that are closely related to each other. Some rain forest macaws are the green-winged macaw, the chestnut-fronted macaw, Buffon's macaw, and the blue and yellow macaw.

Blue and yellow macaws are large birds. They grow up to 33 inches (84 cm) long. They are blue on top and yellow underneath, with black beaks. They live in the rain forests from Panama south to Brazil, Paraguay, and Bolivia. They like to nest in dead trees and are not in great danger of dying out.

Buffon's macaws are also called great green macaws. They grow up to 34 inches (86 cm) long. They are green with a red forehead. They live in the rain forests of Central America, Colombia, and Ecuador.

The largest macaws are the hyacinth macaws. They grow up to 40 inches (102 cm) long. They are deep blue with yellow patches around their eyes. They live in trees near the grasslands of Brazil, the largest country in South America. Only 3,000 remain in the wild. They live both in rain forests and in drier areas.

The smallest macaws are the red-shouldered macaws. They are about 12 inches (30 cm) long. Like all macaws, they have long tails. They prefer to live in the drier areas of northeastern South America rather than in rain forests.

Range and Habitat

Many macaws live in the rain forests of Mexico and Central and South America. Twelve species live in the rain forests of Brazil. They also live on islands off the coast of South America.

Like most birds, macaws live in trees. Macaws can live in many places, including river valleys, swamps, grasslands, and mountain rain forests. Some species like the warmth of tropical areas. These are hot and rainy areas of the world.

Appearance

Macaws are large. They can be many colors, including green, blue, red, or yellow. Unlike many birds, both males and females are colorful. They have short necks, large heads, and very long tails. Macaws also have thick, curved beaks. The beaks of larger macaws are strong enough to snap a broomstick. They use their beaks like people use their hands. They can grab their food or comb each other's feathers with their beaks.

Some macaws have **cheek patches** near their eyes. These patches often have patterns of small feathers. The patches turn pink when macaws are angry, nervous, or excited. The patches are like a person's fingerprints. No two are alike.

▲ **This macaw is using its feet to grasp food and to eat.**

Macaws have four toes on each of their feet. Two toes point forward. The other two point backward. This gives macaws a strong grip. They use their feet to hold food and to grab branches. Like people, macaws are left-handed or right-handed. Unlike people, most macaws are left-handed.

These macaws are eating clay from a riverbank.

What Macaws Eat

Macaws eat nuts, berries, leaves, and seeds. With their strong jaws and beaks, macaws can crack open hard nutshells. They have the strongest bite of any bird. They also use their tongues to dig inside shells to get nuts.

Macaws eat seeds with toxins, or poisons, from soapbox and mahogany trees. These seeds would make many other animals sick, but not macaws. Macaws can eat them because they also eat clay from riverbanks. Macaws visit clay mounds about three times a week. They cling to the clay and scrape chunks into their mouths. If the macaws did not eat the clay, the toxins from the seeds would stay in their bodies. The clay traps the toxins. Then the clay with the toxins passes in the form of **waste**. That means macaws do not get sick.

This macaw is eating fruit from a papaya tree.

Do you know why macaws land in palm trees? The trees have smooth trunks. This helps protect them from some predators. Reptiles and cats cannot climb the smooth trees.

How Macaws Digest Food

Macaws also eat fruit that is not ripe. They like the seeds inside the fruit. Unripe fruit and hard nuts take a long time to digest. Digest means to break down food so the body can use it.

In the clay macaws eat, there are small stones. The stones collect in a part of the body called a **gizzard**. These stones help grind the food macaws eat. This helps the birds digest their food.

How Macaws Find Food

Rain forest trees can grow more than 100 feet (30 meters) tall. In a rain forest, the area of thick leaves and branches high above the ground is called the **canopy**. The canopy has lower, middle, and upper parts. Macaws use their good sense of sight to find nuts and fruit in the canopy.

These two macaws are cleaning each other's feathers.

A Macaw's Life Cycle

Wild macaws can live to be 45 years old. In zoos, these birds can live longer than many humans. They may live to be 70 years old.

Macaws begin to mate when they are about five years old. Like most parrots, macaws stay with the same mate for life. Male and female pairs clean each other's feathers. They touch each other's beaks. They fly so close to each other that their wings almost touch.

Not all female macaws lay eggs every year. When they do lay eggs, most females lay only two eggs per year. Sometimes these eggs do not hatch. If both eggs do hatch, only one chick usually lives to be an adult. The parents only feed one bird. It is either the first chick that hatches or the larger chick.

This female parrot is sitting on eggs in her nest.

Did you know that macaws may have lived as far north as Arizona? Arizona is in the southwest part of the United States. Scientists have found the remains of scarlet macaws there. Remains are what is left of an animal after it dies.

A Macaw's Nest

Usually, the male and female pair builds a nest far from other macaws. They make nests in the holes of dead trees. They put bark and twigs on the bottom of the hole. As soon as the female lays her eggs, the pair stops being **social**. The pair must make sure that other birds do not take over the nest.

Females sit on their eggs from 12 to 35 days. During this time, the male hunts for food. He stores food in a pouch in his throat. He brings it back to the nest to share with the female. When the eggs hatch, both parents take turns hunting for food and feeding the young.

Young

Macaws take care of their chicks for two to three years. Chicks are born blind. Their eyes open after nine to 16 days. Chicks are born without feathers. Fluffy feathers appear in about three weeks. These feathers are called **down** feathers. They are only for warmth. They are not used for flying.

Chicks are not very active. They eat, sleep, and grow. They beg for food by flapping their wings and screeching. They take partly digested fruit and nuts from their parents' mouths. They live in their nests from two to four months. Once they begin to fly, young macaws are called **fledglings**.

Young macaws are in danger from predators. Reptiles, climbing cats, eagles, and other predators attack young macaws when they are in their nests.

This is a young macaw. It is weak and unable to defend itself against predators.

Macaws are social. Like these macaws, the birds usually fly together in groups.

A Macaw's Day

Macaws are very social birds. They like to spend time together. Sometimes there are as many as 100 in a group. They make small clicking sounds to say hello to each other. They are only quiet when they eat or sleep. High in the canopy, macaws are safe from many enemies. The leaves there provide a place to hide from predators. Predators are animals that hunt other animals and eat them. Reptiles and climbing cats are predators that hunt macaws. However, the predators cannot climb high in the canopy. They can only catch macaws that come closer to the forest floor. But even high in the treetops, macaws are not always safe. Harpy eagles hunt them there.

Macaws do not travel far from home. They usually fly to the same places each day. They visit the same trees to look for nuts and fruits.

Macaws rest in the shade during hot afternoons. They use their beaks to pick out dead feathers and parasites. A parasite, such as a tick, is an animal or plant that gets its food from another living thing.

At night, **flocks** meet at a **sleeping tree**. Most sleeping trees stand taller than the trees and bushes around them. They are usually dead trees with no leaves. Macaws argue with each other for the best sleeping spots. In time, they find a good place to spend the night. Since sleeping trees have no leaves, predators have no place to hide. This helps keep macaws safe at night.

These macaws are endangered because of the loss of their rain forest habitat.

How Are Macaws Doing?

All macaw species are either threatened or **endangered**. This means they are in danger of becoming **extinct**. The red Cuban macaw is already extinct. The Glaucous macaw may also be extinct.

People are one of the biggest dangers to macaws. They cut down trees in the rain forests to raise and feed cattle. The macaws need these trees for nesting, for finding food, and for sleeping. Other people use colorful macaw feathers to make special clothing.

Macaws will die without rain forest trees to live in.

Protecting Macaws

Some people also take young macaws from their nests and sell them as pets. Macaws taken from the wild do not make good pets. Many die when they are moved from their habitat. A habitat is a place where an animal or plant usually lives. Macaws taken from their natural home can easily catch diseases or die from the change. Today, laws protect wild macaws. It is against the law to take these birds from their habitats.

Scientists have made macaw **refuges**. A refuge is a place where animals are protected. Macaws are safe in the refuges. When macaws in a refuge lose feathers, scientists collect them. They give the feathers to people who use them for clothing. That way people do not take macaws from the wild.

Many people understand that macaws are important to life in the rain forests. They must teach other people what they know. Together, people of all ages can help keep macaws alive in their rain forest homes for a very long time.

colorful feathers
see page 7

long tail
see page 9

eyes
see page 10

powerful beak
see page 13

feet and claws
see page 11

Glossary

canopy (KAN-uh-pee)—a thick area of leaves and branches high up in the treetops

cheek patch (CHEEK PACH)—special bald spots near a macaw's eyes

down (DOUN)—the soft body feathers of a young bird

endangered (en-DAYN-jurd)—in danger of dying out

extinct (ek-STINGKT)—a species that has died out

fledgling (FLEJ-ling)—a young bird

flock (FLOK)—a group of animals of one kind that live, travel, or feed together

gizzard (GIZ-urd)—a muscular part of a bird's stomach where food is ground

refuge (REF-yooj)—a place where living things are protected or sheltered

sleeping tree (SLEEP-ing TREE)—a special tree where birds spend the night

social (SOH-shuhl)—to live mainly in groups

waste (WAYST)—undigested food that leaves an animal's body in droppings

Internet Sites

Macaws
http://www.ran.org/kids_action/animals.html

Macaw Landing Foundation
http:/www.cnnw.net/~mlf/home.html

Useful Address

National Parrot Association
8 North Hoffman Lane
Hauppauge, NY 11788

Books to Read

Bailey, Jill. *Save the Macaws.* Austin:
  Steck-Vaughn, 1992.

Rauzon, Mark J. *Parrots.* New York: Grolier, 1996.

Index